Nobody Gonna Turn Me 'Round

STORIES AND SONGS OF THE CIVIL RIGHTS MOVEMENT

Doreen Rappaport

illustrated by Shane W. Evans

CANDLEWICK PRESS

ABOUT THIS BOOK

On February 1, 1960, four black college students sat down at a race-segregated lunch counter in Greensboro, North Carolina, demanding to be served. Their actions launched a mass civil rights revolution in the South. I was a teacher at this time, when tens of thousands of black southerners demanded equality and an end to the hideous system of racial segregation. Their courage and dignity in the face of constant violence fired my heart and mind. This book chronicles their struggle from the 1955 Montgomery Bus Boycott until the passage of the Voting Rights Act in July 1965.

Singing inspired, fortified, and unified the civil rights activists as it had their ancestors during slavery and Reconstruction. Song rang out on marches in the streets, at meetings in churches, and in prison cells. I knew "old" versions of many of these freedom songs from my childhood: my father, a vocal arranger, had taught me their importance and beauty. I learned the new words and sang them as powerfully as I could at marches and meetings in the North. The sound of the exhilaration and determination in these songs is still in my ears.

In the summer of 1965, I taught in a freedom school in McComb, Mississippi. There I saw courage and determination firsthand. I was privileged to meet "local heroes"—people whose names were not known beyond their communities, but who are truly American heroes.

As you read this book, remember that this modern civil rights movement did not spring up out of nowhere: it started with the first black resistance when slaves rebelled on slave ships. Every generation found its own way to resist and protest and sustain itself; some times were more difficult than others.

My book includes not-yet-celebrated heroes along with more familiar ones like Dr. Martin Luther King Jr. and Rosa Parks. I searched to tell their stories in the most immediate way possible. I found songs, poems, memoirs, letters, and court testimony and interwove these voices with my own. The dialogue and descriptions of the actions and feelings of Mose Wright, Rosa Parks, Jo Ann Robinson, Elizabeth Eckford, John Lewis, Diane Nash, Fannie Lou Hamer, and Sheyann Webb come directly from their first-person accounts.

This is the last book in a trilogy on the black experience in America for which I have collaborated with artist Shane W. Evans. I have used words to trace the struggles, fears, hopes, inventive resistances, courage, dignity, and triumphs of African Americans starting with the kidnappings 350 years ago through the passage of the 1965 Voting Rights Act. Shane Evans has enriched my text with his expressive paintings.

I think I can safely say that for both of us this has been an enriching and demanding journey. We have learned about many extraordinary people and historical events. But the richness and diversity of this part of American history cannot be contained in three books. I hope our books set you on your journey of discovery about what it means to be free. ▬

Doreen Rappaport

Let a new earth rise. Let another world be born.
Let a bloody peace be written in the sky.
Let a second generation full of courage issue
forth, let a people loving freedom come to
growth. Let a beauty full of healing and a
strength of final clenching be the pulsing in
our spirits and our blood. Let the martial
songs be written, let the dirges disappear.
Let a race of men now rise and take control!

MARGARET WALKER
from "For My People"

W hen the Civil War ended in 1865, newly freed African Americans looked forward to claiming equality. But it was not to be. White southerners devised new laws to deprive them of their rights. Race segregation — separation by race — took hold in the South. WHITE ONLY signs went up at schools, buses, trains, restaurants, libraries, hospitals, and parks. Southern blacks faced daily humiliations, threats, and the possibility of being murdered.

I remember . . .

when my mother's friend dragged me to the rear of the trolley car. — Louis Armstrong

a crowd of armed men cursing my father and forcing him to remove his hat and bow down to them. — Benjamin Mays

how Papa cried like a baby and pleaded at the white hospital that they treat my brother who had been critically injured in an automobile accident. — Chester Himes

seeing the charred bodies of black men.
— Esther Mae Scott

asking Mama, "If the Lord loves everybody, why does he let white folks treat us like this?"
— James Yates

In 1954, a lawsuit filed by the National Association for the Advancement of Colored People (NAACP) challenging school segregation came before the U.S. Supreme Court. In *Brown v. Board of Education of Topeka, Kansas,* the nine justices unanimously declared school segregation unconstitutional.

The decision was so overwhelming that for a while we all just sat there looking at one another. The only emotion we felt at the moment was awe — every one of us felt it.

Roy Wilkins
Executive Secretary, NAACP

The joy of black Americans, however, was short-lived. New hate groups sprang up. The Ku Klux Klan donned white hoods and robes and burned crosses on the lawns of "nigger troublemakers." One hundred southern congressmen denounced the Supreme Court decision and urged whites to disobey the ruling.

The lives of black southern activists were fragile. In May 1955, Reverend George W. Lee and Lamar Smith, NAACP organizers in Mississippi, were murdered for trying to register black voters. Their murders received little attention.

In August 1955, Emmett Till, a fourteen-year-old Chicagoan, went to visit his great-uncle in Money, Mississippi. His mother warned him: "Be careful how you speak. Say 'yes, sir' and 'no, ma'am.' Do not hesitate to humble yourself if you have to get down on your knees."

A few days into his vacation, Till went into Bryant's grocery to buy bubble gum. When leaving, he whistled and said, "Bye, Baby" to Mrs. Bryant.

His friends laughed. "Bobo, don't you know you're not supposed to say goodbye to a white woman?" Three days later, Till's mangled body was pulled out of the river.

The news that a fourteen-year-old boy had been murdered for speaking "improperly" to a white woman in Mississippi flashed across the country.

Before Emmett Till's murder, I had known the fear of hunger, hell, and the Devil. But now there was a new fear known to me — the fear of being killed just because I was black. I didn't know what one had to do or not do as a Negro not to be killed.

Anne Moody, age 15
Centerville, Mississippi

Till's mother wanted the world "to see what they had done to my boy." More than fifty thousand people marched by his open casket. Thousands fainted or cried upon seeing his bloated, bashed-in face. Tens of thousands more saw photographs of what was left of his face in *Jet* magazine. Black Americans were horrified. So were many white Americans. Not even children were safe from southern racists.

Two white men, J.W. Milam and Roy Bryant, were charged with the murder. They were not worried, for who would dare testify against them? Certainly not anyone black.

The Story of Mose Wright

Ceiling fans whir hot, humid air about the courtroom. People jam the entrance doors. Black men and women are frisked for weapons; only the first forty are let in. Four black reporters are allowed to enter, but they are forbidden to sit with the seventy white reporters covering the trial.

"Mose Wright." The name rings out in the segregated courtroom. The judge puts down his bottle of soda and looks up.

Sixty-four-year-old Wright feels hundreds of unfriendly eyes glare at him as he walks across the room. White people frown and roll their eyes in disgust as he settles into the witness box. Wright has been in hiding since the night Till was taken from his house. He has been warned that he will be killed if he testifies. In his whole life, he has never once spoken up against a white man, but he is determined to tell the truth today.

The prosecutor asks Wright directly, "Can you identify the men who took Emmett Till from your home?"

"There he is," Wright says. He stands up and points to J. W. Milam.

Milam leans forward, lit cigarette in his mouth. Wright feels the hatred in his eyes.

"And there's Mr. Bryant," Wright says.

"Order, order!" The judge pounds his gavel, but
there is no need, for there is only stunned silence
in the courtroom. ▬

Two other black Mississippians — Willie Reed and
Amanda Bradley — testified against the defendants. The
all-white male jury deliberated for only seventy-two
minutes and declared Milam and Bryant "not guilty."
Immediately after the trial, Mose Wright, Willie Reed,
and Amanda Bradley fled Mississippi, but southern blacks
never forgot their courage in testifying.

On Thursday, December 1, 1955, black activist Rosa Parks spontaneously challenged segregation on a bus in Montgomery, Alabama.

The Story of Rosa Parks

Rosa Parks drops ten cents into the fare box. She glances at the bus driver. He looks familiar. Oh, yes. She knows that face. Twelve years ago, he put her off a bus when she refused to enter by the back door. She takes a seat right behind the section reserved for whites.

At the next stop, more white passengers get on. When one of them cannot find a seat, the driver calls out, "Let me have those seats." Rosa and every other black person know they are expected to give up their seats. No one moves.

"Y'all better make it light on yourselves and let me have those seats," he calls out again.

Make it light on us, Rosa thinks. *What a joke. The more we give in, the worse they treat us.*

Two black women get up. So does the black man next to Rosa. Rosa slides over, taking his seat.

"Are you going to move?" the bus driver demands.

Rosa looks up at him. "No." She speaks softly but firmly.

"Well then, I'm going to have you arrested."

"You may do that," she answers calmly. She knows she may be thrown in jail. Or beaten. But

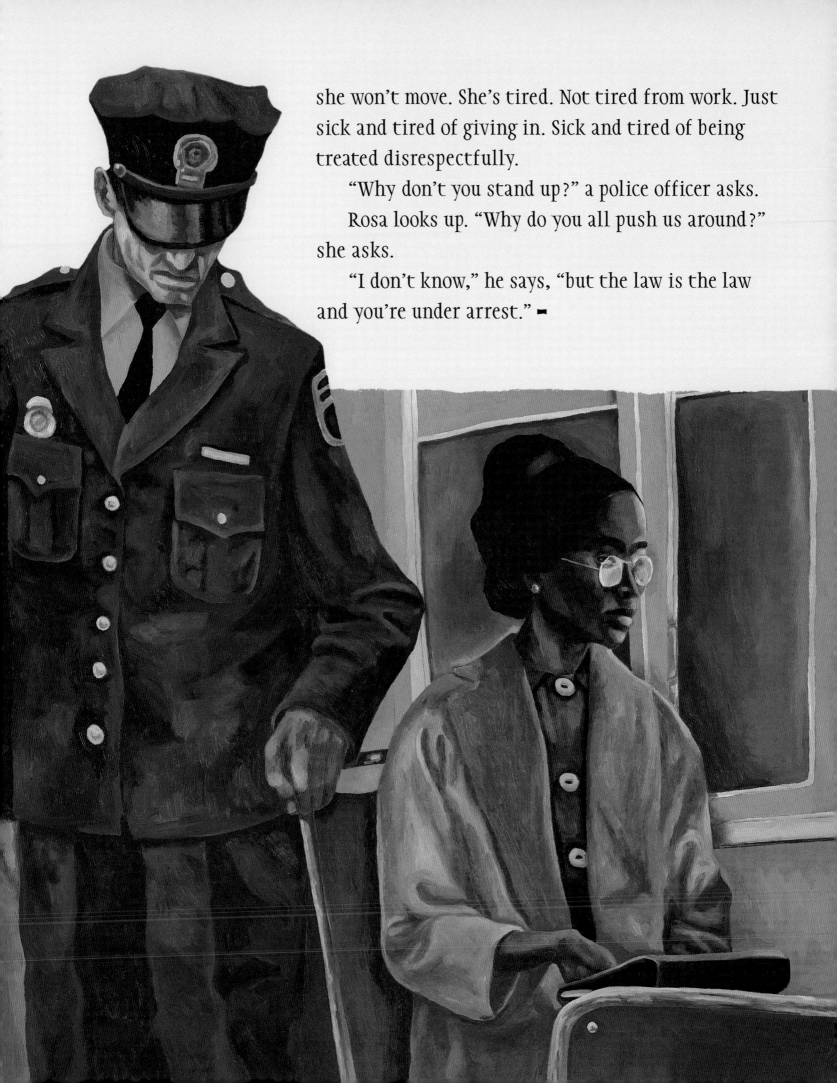

she won't move. She's tired. Not tired from work. Just sick and tired of giving in. Sick and tired of being treated disrespectfully.

"Why don't you stand up?" a police officer asks.

Rosa looks up. "Why do you all push us around?" she asks.

"I don't know," he says, "but the law is the law and you're under arrest." ▪

The Story of Jo Ann Robinson

College professor and activist Jo Ann Robinson learns of Parks's arrest. She knows that this is the moment the Women's Political Council of Montgomery has been waiting for. Now is the time for a bus boycott. Within an hour, a friend and two students join her, and the mimeograph machine is whirring:

Another Negro woman has been arrested and thrown into jail because she refused to get up out of her seat on the bus for a white person. This has to be stopped. Negroes have rights, too. If we do not do something to stop these arrests, the next time it may be you, or your daughter, or mother. We are, therefore, asking every Negro to stay off the buses Monday in protest of the arrest and trial.

The list of what to do is endless, and they have only seventy-two hours to organize the details:

• Feed the machine with paper — 17,500 sheets.

• Cut each printed sheet in thirds.

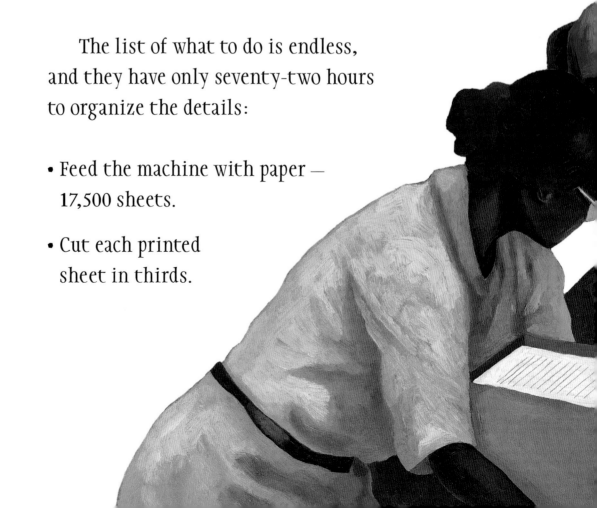

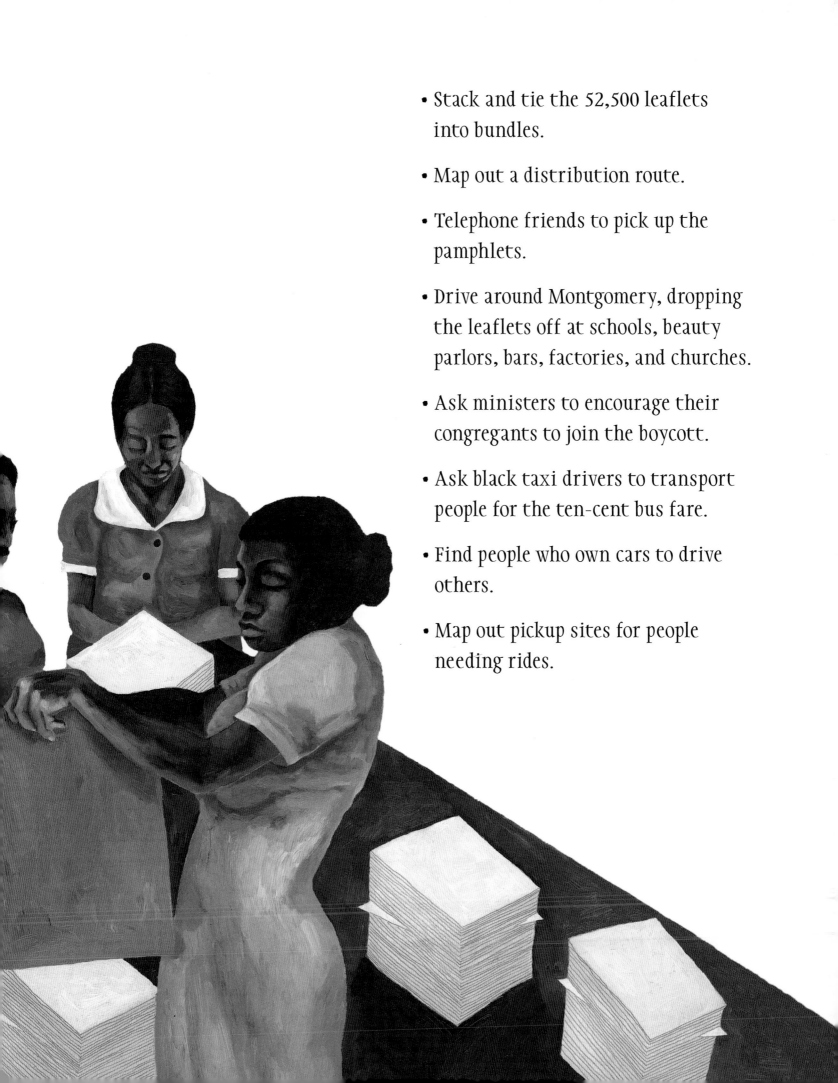

- Stack and tie the 52,500 leaflets into bundles.

- Map out a distribution route.

- Telephone friends to pick up the pamphlets.

- Drive around Montgomery, dropping the leaflets off at schools, beauty parlors, bars, factories, and churches.

- Ask ministers to encourage their congregants to join the boycott.

- Ask black taxi drivers to transport people for the ten-cent bus fare.

- Find people who own cars to drive others.

- Map out pickup sites for people needing rides.

On Monday morning, December 5, 1955, the empty buses clanked along. That evening, six thousand people packed the Holt Street Baptist Church and spilled over onto the three blocks on either side. "This is just the beginning!" someone shouted as they voted yes to continuing the boycott.

The Montgomery Improvement Association (MIA) was formed. A new minister in town, twenty-six-year-old Dr. Martin Luther King Jr., was chosen as leader. King believed that nonviolent direct action, like this boycott, could change life for black Americans. That night at a mass meeting, he reminded his audience that "one of the great glories of democracy is the right to protest for right."

For 381 days, Montgomery's fifty thousand black citizens carpooled or walked everywhere — to work, school, church, and to visit friends and relatives. Sunday collection boxes jingled with coins to pay for gas and tires and car repairs.

Neither rain, hail, sleet, unrelenting heat, harassment, loss of jobs, nor bombings stopped them. Twice a week, people buttressed their determination at large meetings. In this first mass action of the civil rights revolution, song and prayer unified and strengthened the boycotters as it had their slave ancestors worshiping in secret and their families trying to survive under segregation.

Ain't gonna ride them buses no more,

Ain't gonna ride no more.

Why don't all the white folk know

That I ain't gonna ride no more.

On November 13, 1956, the U.S. Supreme Court ruled that bus segregation was illegal. On December 21, 1956, Montgomery's black citizens began riding the buses again. White segregationists retaliated. Snipers fired at buses and bombed five black churches and the homes of three black ministers. Black clergy formed the Southern Christian Leadership Conference (SCLC) and elected Dr. King as its president.

The Supreme Court had declared in May 1954 that the schools were to be desegregated with "all deliberate speed," but school integration in the South progressed at a snail's pace. In September 1957, nine black teenagers signed up to go to the newly integrated Central High in Little Rock, Arkansas. The night before school opened, the governor of Arkansas warned on television: "Blood will run in the streets if Negro pupils attempt to enter Central High School." NAACP leader Daisy Bates arranged a police escort to drive the teenagers to school. She never reached Elizabeth Eckford. The next morning, the fifteen-year-old set off alone.

The Story of Elizabeth Eckford

Off the bus. Down the street. Elizabeth is startled to see a mob of jeering whites and hundreds of white guardsmen with guns ringing Central High. The school is only a block away. But that block looks longer than any she has ever seen. *Maybe I'll be safe if I walk to the front entrance where the guards are*, she thinks.

With her every step, hateful words pierce her ears. She sees a National Guardsman letting white students into the school. *If I get to the guards, they will protect me.* But when she reaches the door, a guard blocks her way. She tries to squeeze past him. Up goes his rifle. Up go the rifles of the other white guardsmen.

A woman spits at her.

"Get her! Lynch her!"

Elizabeth retreats to the bus stop. Ugly words follow her. *Please, bus, come.* More ugly words. She cannot control the tears streaming down her cheeks.

A white northern reporter puts his arm around her. "Don't let them see you cry," he says softly.

"Get a rope and drag her to a tree!"

"Leave this child alone!" a white woman shouts. "Why are you tormenting her? Six months from now, you will hang your heads in shame."

"Another nigger-lover! Get her out of here!"

The white woman takes Elizabeth's arm and leads her through the screaming mob to home and safety. ▬

For fourteen days, rioting whites kept the nine teenagers out of school. Daisy Bates asked President Dwight D. Eisenhower for help. Finally, he ordered one thousand federal marshals with bayonets to escort the students into school. For two months, bodyguards followed them from class to class. When the soldiers left, the abuse resumed for the rest of the year. In the next ten years, riots flared when other black southerners integrated white schools.

Ernest Green, the oldest of the nine students, graduated in May 1958.
Soldiers were stationed all about the auditorium when he claimed his diploma.
Poet Langston Hughes named Green the Man of the Year:

The blood of young black men and women beaten by overseers until their backs
were raw for daring to study in secret is soaked into the paper of that diploma.
The tears of slave mothers who desperately wanted their children to learn
moisten all the letters on Ernest Green's diploma. It is the diploma
of all the people who remember grandfathers and grandmothers
who did not know how to read and write because they never
had a chance to learn, for whom the barriers to learning
were too high, or the terrors in the way too great.

John Lewis is the son of a sharecropper from Troy, Alabama. In September 1958, he was studying at American Baptist Theological Seminary in Nashville, Tennessee. He attended workshops on nonviolence held by James Lawson. Lawson was a thirty-one-year-old Methodist minister. Like Martin Luther King Jr., Lawson believed that nonviolent direct action as practiced by Mahatma Gandhi in India could end race segregation.

The Story of John Lewis

John Lewis listens attentively as Lawson reads from the New Testament: "Jesus read, 'The Spirit of the Lord is upon me, because he hath anointed me to preach the gospel to the poor; he hath sent me to heal the brokenhearted, to preach deliverance to the captives.'"

It is all there in the text. Jesus brought the message of deliverance to "the captives." Lewis understands that Lawson is saying that black people living under segregation are captives. So are white people, trapped in their hate. It is up to John and his friends to break this ugly cycle of hate. By using the power of love, they will help each other and help others. They will forgive their enemies as Jesus did, and that will bring them the courage to face whatever is ahead.

John looks about the room. Bernard Lafayette, another ministerial student, is here. So is Paul La Prad, a Quaker from the Midwest. There are fewer than twenty people, and they are all young. How can so few heal Americans of their hate? How can they create a different America when so many others have failed? ▪

The tactic chosen to break segregation was sit-ins. The first target would be department store restaurants. The students would sit in a "white-only" section and demand equal service. Lawson knew that segregationists would respond violently to this nonviolent action. In role-playing sessions, the students learned how to protect themselves.

The Story of Diane Nash

Diane Nash, a first-year student at Fisk University, holds a book up to her face as if she is reading. John Lewis and Bernard Lafayette strut back and forth behind her. John is her friend, and so is Bernard, but the echo of their steps on the wooden floor sounds dangerous. "Go back to Africa, nigger!" they shout. *Nigger.* The ugliest of all words rings in her ears. *It's only a word. It can't hurt you.*

The power of the ugly word subsides.

Lafayette suddenly grabs her arm. Her hands shoot up to protect her head as she falls to the floor. She rolls into a knot, keeping her knees close to her head. It's only pretend, yet it feels so real. Lewis mock-kicks her side and lowers a broom toward her back. She can't do this. It's too dangerous. Then she remembers what James Lawson said: When Jesus was confronted by an angry mob set on killing him, he did not fight back. He "walked through the midst" of them. She can "walk through the midst" of this.

Her fear subsides. ▬

Diane Nash overcame her fear when it was her time to sit-in and be arrested. She emerged as a leader in the movement.

In Greensboro, North Carolina, four black students at North Carolina Agricultural and Technical College were also debating challenging segregation. On February 1, 1960, David Richmond, Franklin McCain, Ezell Blair Jr., and Joseph McNeil sat down at a segregated lunch counter in F. W. Woolworth's Department Store.

"May we have some coffee?"

"Sorry, we don't serve colored here," replied the waitress.

They sat at the lunch counter until Woolworth's closed. The next day, twenty other A&T students came with them. Three days later, white women from the University of North Carolina Women's College joined them.

Sympathetic northerners—black and white—picketed Woolworth's in their own cities, asking people not to shop there until the southern stores were integrated.

Within weeks, the sit-in movement spread across the South. By April 1960, seventy thousand black southerners had protested in seventy-eight cities.

Ev'ry body sing Freedom,

Free - dom,

Free - dom,

Free - dom, Free - dom.

Activist Ella Baker encouraged an interracial group of sit-in students to band together. The Student Nonviolent Coordinating Committee (SNCC, pronounced "Snick") was born.

Tens of thousands of black southerners joined the sit-in movement. They protested all over the South — Cambridge, Maryland; Nashville, Tennessee; Albany, Georgia; Atlanta, Georgia; Jackson, Mississippi; Talladega, Alabama; Orangeburg, South Carolina; Danville, Virginia; Durham, North Carolina; and Jacksonville, Florida.

The civil rights activists
sat-in restaurants,
read-in libraries,
slept-in hotel lobbies,
stood-in movie houses,
waded-in municipal pools,
prayed-in city halls, and
knelt-in white churches.

Angry whites
cursed them,
spat at them,
threw ammonia in their faces,
poured pepper over their heads,
ground lit cigarettes into their backs,
yanked them off lunch counters,
pummeled them with fists,
swung baseball bats and ax handles,
threw bricks and stones,
and bombed their churches and homes.
The activists never raised their fists.

Police officers swung billy clubs,
sprayed tear gas,
buzzed electric prods, and
set attack dogs on them,
then arrested them for
"marching without a permit"
or "disturbing the peace"
or "trespassing."

Police shoved them,
dragged them,
and herded them like cattle
into vans off to jail.
Federal officials stood on the
sidelines and watched.
The demonstrators never raised
their fists.

The activists telegraphed
the U.S. attorney general
and the FBI director

and the Justice Department

and the President

to help stop the violence.

Help rarely came.

Their lawyers argued

that *they* were the victims,

but southern white judges

sentenced them to work gangs

and state penitentiaries

and solitary confinement.

And they filled the jails with song.

DOREEN RAPPAPORT

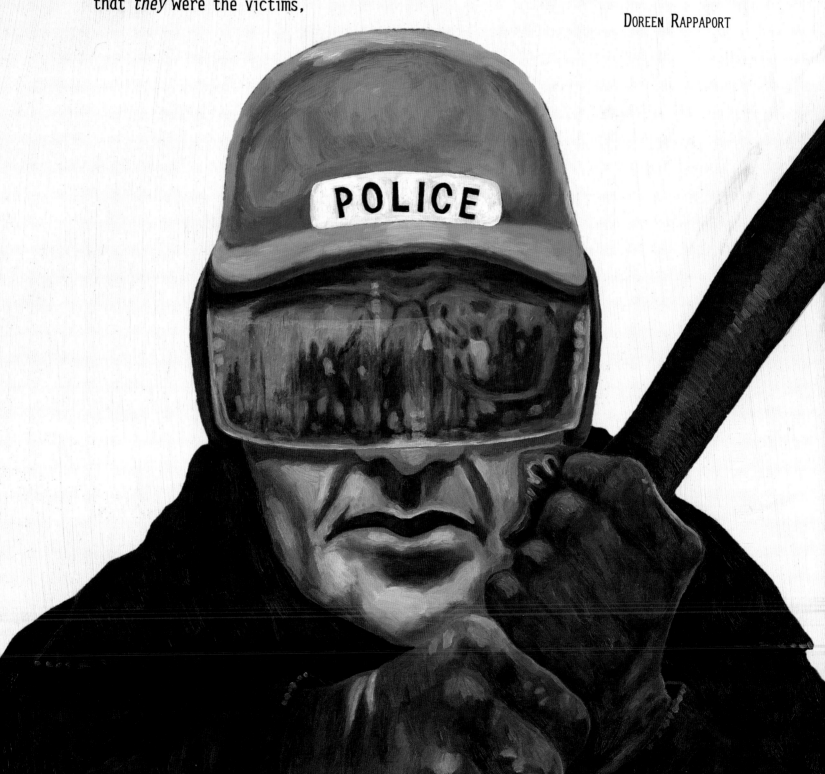

New words for spirituals, hymns, and blues were constantly being written to fit each situation. Outside the Nashville courthouse, twenty-five hundred blacks sang "Everybody Sing Freedom" to the tune of the spiritual "Amen" in support of the students inside on trial. In Albany, Georgia, Bernice Johnson surprised herself in jail when she spontaneously changed a phrase in an old spiritual, "Over my head, I see trouble in the air," to "Over my head, I see freedom in the air." Alice Wine from John Island, South Carolina, rewrote the lyrics, "Keep your hand on the plow" to "Keep your eyes on the prize."

No longer hiding in the "hush harbors," black southerners sang out forcefully and joyfully. Clapping, stomping, swaying, they sang together to affirm their determination. They were leading themselves out of Egypt, leading themselves out of the imprisonment of segregation and injustice. Their courage transformed them, and so did their singing.

Keep Your Eyes on the Prize

1. Paul and Si - las, bound in jail, ___ had no mo-ney for to go their bail, __ Keep your eyes on the prize,

Hold __ on, hold on. Hold _____ on, _____ Hold ___ on, _____ Keep your ___ eyes on ___ the prize, _____ Hold ___ on, hold on.

2. We're gonna ride for civil rights,
   we're gonna ride for both black and white.
   Keep your eyes on the prize, hold on.

3. We've met jail and violence too,
   but God's love has seen us through.
   Keep your eyes on the prize, hold on.

James Farmer was the founder of a northern civil rights group, the Congress of Racial Equality (CORE). In May 1961, CORE began a series of "Freedom Rides" by interracial groups on public buses through the Deep South. The purpose was to test a Supreme Court ruling that segregation was illegal on interstate buses and railroads and their facilities. Violence met the riders at every stop. John Lewis was on the first ride. Never once were those wielding weapons arrested, but in the course of many freedom rides, more than 300 freedom riders were jailed for "disturbing the peace." James Farmer was sentenced to Parchman Prison, a maximum security facility in Mississippi.

As a way of keeping our spirits up, we sang freedom songs. The prison officials said, "If you don't stop singing, we'll take away your mattresses." Now, the mattresses were the only convenience we had in those little cells. Everything else was cold and hard, and the mattress was no more than an inch and a half thick, and straw, but at least it was something. People were quiet for a while, until finally Jim Bevel pointed out, "What they're trying to do is take your soul away. It's not the mattress, it's your soul." Then everybody said, "Yes, yes, we'll keep our soul." One Freedom Rider then yelled, "Guards, guards, guards," and the guards came dashing out to the cellblock to see what was wrong. He said, "Come get my mattress. I'll keep my soul." And everybody started singing. They came in and took the mattresses away and people sang as they had never sung before.

In November 1961, the Interstate Commerce Commission ended segregation on interstate buses and railroads and in their facilities.

Some black northerners, such as James Farmer and Robert Parris Moses, were drawn south to participate in the movement. Bob Moses was teaching math at a private high school in New York City when he read about the sit-ins. When he saw photographs of the demonstrators, he saw himself in their faces. He went south and became a SNCC field worker in Mississippi.

Some black Americans took another route in protest. Heavyweight champion of the world Cassius Clay joined the Nation of Islam, a largely northern urban movement. He changed his name to Muhammad Ali. Ali followed the teachings of Elijah Muhammad, who preached black pride and separatism from whites. Elijah Muhammad's emphasis on black superiority and independence threatened most white Americans.

Another prominent black Muslim was Malcolm X. Malcolm X was a school dropout and drug user until he was sent to prison, where he became a follower of Elijah Muhammad. Malcolm X was a brilliant orator and organizer and recruited thousands of northern black men and women into the Nation of Islam. For many years, Malcolm X called white people "devils" and attacked the civil rights movement as irrelevant. But while traveling through Africa and the Middle East, he met whites who had no prejudice. He began to rethink his antagonisms and spoke of a new generation of whites and blacks as the hope of America.

In April 1963, Reverend Fred Shuttlesworth of Birmingham, Alabama, set out on a campaign to desegregate the stores in the downtown. He asked Dr. King to join the struggle. The jails rapidly filled with adults, including Drs. King and Shuttlesworth. White judges ordered the demonstrations stopped. When the number of adult demonstrators thinned, activist James Bevel organized children to march.

Seated in the comfort of their homes in front of their televisions, people all over the world were horrified by images of snarling police dogs tearing children's clothing, fire hoses blasting them into trees, and police beating them with clubs — all because they wanted the right to eat at a lunch counter. More than two thousand children, some as young as seven, were hauled off to jail.

Oh Freedom

Oh _____ Free-dom   Oh _____ Free-dom

Oh _____ free-dom o - ver me   o - ver me,__ and be -

fore I'll be a slave __   I'll be bur-ied in my grave ___ and go __

home   to my   Lord __   and be   free.

On May 10, merchants agreed to desegregate lunch counters and hire blacks. That night, bombs exploded at the home of Dr. King's younger brother and at the motel where Dr. King was staying. Long-simmering black frustration erupted into rioting; white police met the rioters with force. President Kennedy finally took action and sent federal soldiers to a fort near Birmingham. The city quieted, and the agreement held.

A month later, President John F. Kennedy sent a civil rights bill to Congress. It protected voting rights, banned segregation in public places, and denied federal funds to any program excluding or segregating blacks. Civil rights leaders were determined the bill pass. Labor leader A. Philip Randolph planned a March on Washington for Jobs and Freedom.

On August 28, 1963, a quarter of a million people —black, white, young, and old —filled the streets of the nation's capital. They came by bus and train and car and plane from all over the United States. Some people walked long distances. It was the single largest protest ever in the capital. The air rang out with freedom songs.

By now, "We Shall Overcome" was the unofficial anthem of the civil rights movement.

We Shall Overcome

We shall o - ver come,_____ We shall o - ver - come,___ We shall o - ver - come some - day._____

__ Oh,___ deep in my heart, (I know that)*

I do be-lieve (oh____)* We shall o - ver-come some - day.

* not part of original song

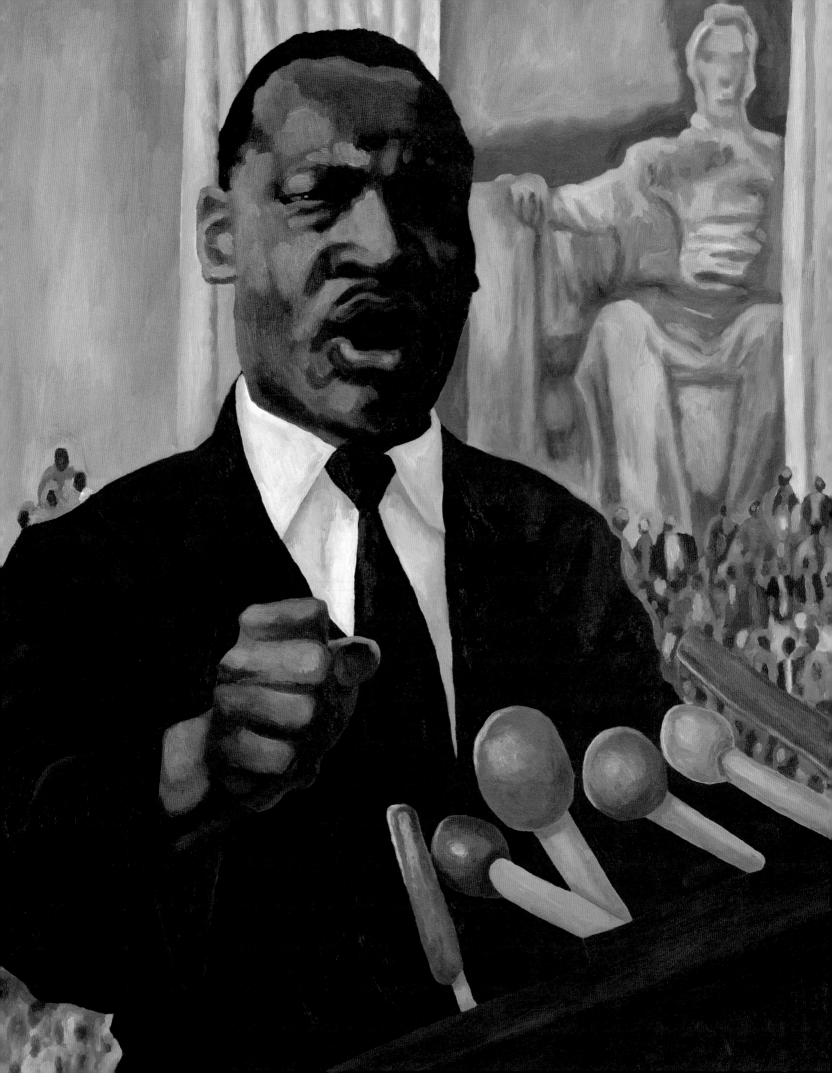

The official program at the Lincoln Memorial opened with Marian Anderson, the great contralto, singing the national anthem. There were speeches by labor leaders and religious leaders and activists from SNCC and CORE and the NAACP. Television brought Martin Luther King Jr.'s glorious vision to eighty million Americans; most had never heard him speak before.

I have a dream. It is a dream deeply rooted in the American dream. I have a dream that one day this nation will rise up and live out the true meaning of its creed, "We hold these truths to be self-evident, that all men are created equal."

I have a dream that one day on the red hills of Georgia, the sons of former slaves and the sons of former slaveowners will be able to sit down together at the table of brotherhood.

I have a dream that my four little children will one day live in a nation where they will not be judged by the color of their skin but by the content of their character.

I have a dream that one day, down in Alabama, little black boys and black girls will be able to join hands with little white boys and white girls as sisters and brothers.

I have a dream today.

Eighteen days after the march, a bomb set at the Sixteenth Street Baptist Church in Birmingham, Alabama, killed four girls at a Bible study class.

In November, President Kennedy was assassinated. President Lyndon Johnson pressed Congress to pass the Civil Rights Bill. Black activists had few expectations about these new laws, for there were already so many other laws that southern whites defied.

As the movement spread, activists focused on securing the vote. African Americans made up forty-five percent of Mississippians, but only five percent were registered to vote. Threats, poll taxes, qualifying tests, and the possibility of being murdered kept southern blacks from voting.

Fannie Lou Hamer was a sharecropper and timekeeper on a cotton plantation in Ruleville. One August evening, she attended a mass meeting at a church where SNCC workers talked about voting.

The Story of Fannie Lou Hamer

—

"This little light of mine.
 I'm gonna let it shine,
  let it shine, let it shine, let it shine."

The church fills with song, and Fannie Lou Hamer's weariness from ten hours in the cotton fields lifts. She throws her head back and opens her eyes. They gleam with passion and hope. She sways and claps her hands. Her powerful voice shakes the timbers and stimulates others to sing. She smiles at the SNCC workers. They look so young. Young enough to be her sons.

"We'll help you register to vote," says Bob Moses in a soft-spoken voice.

Fannie Lou Hamer wants to vote. She's always wanted to vote. But this is the first time she has ever heard about voter registration. Most nights she's too tired to listen to the radio, where you might learn about such things. After ten hours of picking cotton, she's too tired to do much of anything.

Bob Moses talks for a while. Then James Bevel, a fiery young man, speaks. The more these young men talk, the more she senses that she can ask them anything, and they won't laugh at her if her talk isn't "proper."

No doubt about it. She is going down to register. And when she gets that vote, she's going to vote out all those white people who don't care about black people or poor people.

The white registrar "flunks" Hamer and seventeen others on the "qualifying" test. Driving home, they are arrested for traveling in a bus painted the "wrong color yellow."

Hamer finds her employer of eighteen years waiting for her at home. Before Marlowe speaks, she sees the rage in his eyes.

"Fannie Lou, you have been to the courthouse to try to register," he says. "We are not ready for this in Mississippi."

She knows Marlowe is serious. She knows there will be repercussions from her decision, but there is no way she is going to withdraw. "I didn't go down there to register for you," she says. "I went down there to register for myself."

"I will give you until tomorrow morning to withdraw. If you don't, you will have to leave this place."

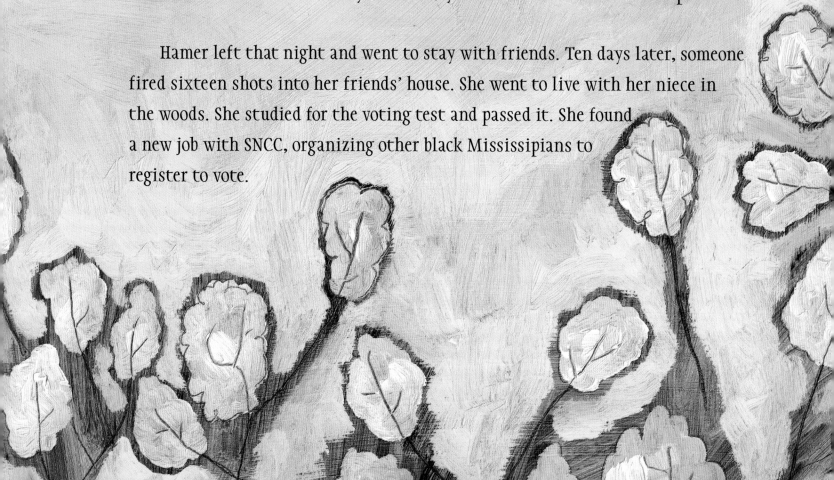

Hamer left that night and went to stay with friends. Ten days later, someone fired sixteen shots into her friends' house. She went to live with her niece in the woods. She studied for the voting test and passed it. She found a new job with SNCC, organizing other black Mississipians to register to vote.

In 1961, a coalition of civil rights groups set up the Council of Federated Organizations (COFO). In the fall of 1963 a Freedom Vote campaign was created. In a mock election, a slate of candidates ran against regular Republican and Democratic candidates. NAACP leader Aaron Henry ran for governor; Ed King, a white chaplain from Tougaloo College, ran for lieutenant governor. White students from Yale and Stanford came for two weeks to help COFO workers bring out the vote. On November 3, 4, and 5, 1963, more than 83,000 blacks voted at makeshift polls at churches, cafés, beauty parlors, groceries, and pool halls. Here was proof that if allowed to, black Mississippians would vote in great numbers.

COFO established a community-based political party called the Mississippi Freedom Democratic Party (MFDP). In August 1964 the MFDP, with its own slate of candidates, challenged the legality of the all-white Mississippi delegation at the Democratic Convention. Fannie Lou Hamer spoke of the violence against black Mississippians who dared to challenge segregation. She wept describing how she was beaten for daring to attend a civil rights meeting. "If the Freedom Democratic Party is not seated now, I question America," said Hamer. "Is this the land of the free and the home of the brave where we have to sleep with our telephones off the hook, because our lives be threatened daily?"

The Democratic Party offered a compromise of two seats on the Mississippi delegation. The MFDP refused because they felt that accepting the compromise would betray the black citizens of Mississippi, who had risked so much trying to register to vote.

During Freedom Summer 1964, the Council of Federated Organizations recruited eight hundred northern college students to help register black voters in Mississippi. A few days after their arrival, three civil rights workers disappeared. A month later, their bodies were found buried in an earthen dam.

The murders made national headlines. Black activists knew that the attention came from the deaths of the two white northerners, not the death of the black Mississippian James Chaney, a twenty-one-year-old CORE worker. CORE worker Dave Dennis expressed his outrage in his eulogy for Chaney:

> *I want to talk about the living dead, not only here in the state of Mississippi, but throughout the nation. Those are the people who don't care. And those who do care but don't have the guts enough to stand up for it. And those people who are busy up in Washington and other places using my freedom and my life to play politics with. That includes the president on down to the governor of the state of Mississippi.*
>
> *I not only blame the people who pulled the trigger or did the beating or dug the hole with the shovel. I blame the people in Washington, D.C., and on down in the state of Mississippi for what happened just as much as I blame those who pulled the trigger.*
>
> *I'm sick and tired of going to funerals of black men who have been murdered by white men.*
>
> *I've got vengeance in my heart tonight, and I ask you to feel angry with me. I'm sick and tired, and I ask you to be sick and tired with me. I'm tired of the people of this country allowing this thing to continue to happen.*

On July 2, 1964, President Lyndon B. Johnson signed the Civil Rights Act prohibiting discrimination in public accomodations and in employment. But the violence against black southerners did not stop.

In 1964, Mississippi had no compulsory education law. Funding for white schools was four times that for black schools. During Freedom Summer, more than two thousand children attended forty-one freedom schools. They were taught by northern whites and blacks: many were teachers during the school year. Children learned foreign languages, creative writing, mathematics, and the proud history of their people. They wrote and performed plays. Their poems and memoirs were published in the SNCC newsletter, *The Student Voice.* In McComb, fear of white retaliation initially made black clergy refuse to let the freedom school meet in a church. Sixteen-year-old Joyce Brown reprimanded her elders:

I asked for your churches, and you turned me down,

But I'll do my work if I have to do it on the ground,

You will not speak for fear of being heard,

So you crawl in your shell and say, "Do not disturb,"

You think because you've turned me away,

You've protected yourself for another day.

But tomorrow surely will come,

And your enemy will still be there with the rising sun,

He'll be there tomorrow as all tomorrows in the past,

And he'll follow you into the future if you let him pass.

Her powerful words opened the churches.

The church elders had not been mistaken about the danger. In the next three months, there were 1,000 arrests, 80 beatings, 35 shootings, 37 black church bombings, and 30 bombings of black homes in Mississippi.

When the movement came to Selma, Alabama, eight-year-old Sheyann Webb found herself marching with six hundred other people on Sunday, March 7, 1965. At the Pettus Bridge, the troops ordered them to stop. They refused, and state troopers, under order from Alabama Governor George Wallace, attacked.

The Story of Sheyann Webb

—

"God, they're killing us!" Hysterical cries surround Sheyann.

Run, run away from the mounted police officers with face masks, swinging whips, and clubs.

Push. Stumble. Bodies jam together as people desperately try to get over the bridge.

Run, run. She's got to get away before she is whipped. But she can't move. Her body is frozen.

"Let's pray," someone says. Sheyann kneels. More pushing. More screaming. Dogs barking. Sirens wailing. Police everywhere, charging on horseback. Suddenly a thick gray cloud of gas surrounds her. *Get up. Get up.* She finds her feet and starts running. The gas is burning her eyes, and she can't see. But behind her she hears whips swishing and horses' hooves and the cries of people being hit. *I'm going to die. I'm going to be trampled to death.*

Then somebody lifts her under her arms and starts running with her. It's Reverend Hosea Williams.

She kicks her legs. "Put me down! You can't run fast enough with me."

But he holds on to her and keeps running until they are a few blocks over on the other side of the bridge and safe — at least for now. ■

At a mass meeting that night, the mood was solemn until the singing began. Someone started singing new words to "Nobody Gonna Turn Me 'Round." And then, once again the community felt their strength. No one could stop them singing. No one could stop them marching. They had not been defeated, and they would triumph.

Ain't Gonna Let Nobody Turn Me 'Round

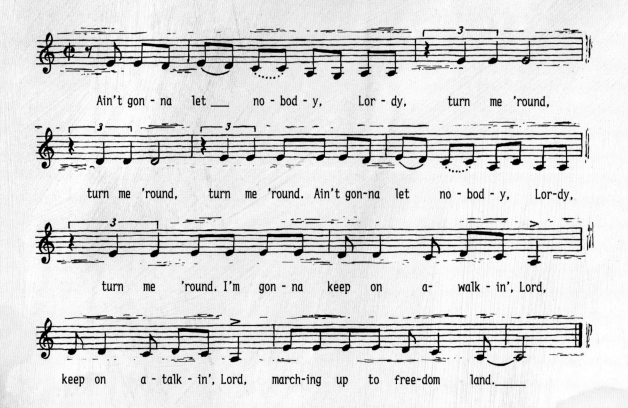

Ain't gon - na let___ no - bod - y, Lor - dy, turn me 'round, turn me 'round, turn me 'round. Ain't gon-na let no - bod - y, Lor-dy, turn me 'round. I'm gon - na keep on a- walk - in', Lord, keep on a - talk - in', Lord, march-ing up to free-dom land.___

Ain't gonna let George Wallace, Lordy,
turn me 'round, turn me 'round, turn me 'round.
Ain't gonna let George Wallace, Lordy, turn me 'round.
I'm gonna keep on a-walkin', Lord,
keep on a-talkin', Lord, marching up to freedom land.

Again television brought the brutal attacks on southern black citizens into millions of American living rooms. People were horrified that police officers had assaulted peaceful demonstrators, and they responded with demonstrations in more than eighty cities.

Dr. King asked religious leaders to come to Selma to complete the march. Hundreds of Americans from all parts of the United States came. Jim Reeb, a white minister who heeded the call, was beaten to death on a Selma street before he even marched.

There were two more marches before the thirty thousand demonstrators were able to cross the bridge and walk the fifty-five miles to the state capital. For that third march, President Lyndon B. Johnson had nationalized the Alabama National Guard, allowing the demonstrators to complete their peaceful walk without being attacked. That night after the march, however, a white activist from Detroit named Viola Liuzzo was shot on the highway by Klan members.

Ten days later, President Lyndon Johnson presented his Voting Rights Bill to Congress. "It is not just Negroes. All of us must overcome the crippling legacy of bigotry and injustice," he told lawmakers. "And we shall overcome."

Six months later, the bill became law. The long, hard battle for the vote for southern blacks was over. No longer could white southern registrars "test" blacks on their state constitution. No longer could they discriminate against potential black voters. The new law finally guaranteed the power of the vote to southern black men and women. Nonviolence had triumphed.

JIM LAWSON

JOHN LEWIS

BERNARD LAFAYETTE

BERNICE JOHNSON REAGON

For fifteen years, tens of thousands of black southerners risked their lives to desegregate the South and to secure equal protection before the law and the right to vote, already guaranteed by the Constitution. The toll of their campaign: forty people murdered and thousands jailed and beaten.

The passage of the Voting Rights Act did not end the civil rights movement, nor did it end violence against black Americans. Activists are still working to make America live up to its promise of equality for all.

We shall overcome . . .

Jim Lawson is still giving workshops on how nonviolence can change the world.

We shall overcome . . .

Since 1986, John Lewis has served the people of the Fifth Congressional District of Georgia in the U.S. Congress.

We shall overcome . . .

Bernard Lafayette is the director of Peace Studies and scholar in residence at the University of Rhode Island.

We shall overcome . . .

Musicologist Bernice Johnson Reagon formed an all-woman *a capella* group, Sweet Honey in the Rock. It uses song and story to bring hope to people everywhere.

We shall overcome . . .

Fred Shuttlesworth is now a minister in Cincinnati, Ohio.

We shall overcome . . .

Bob Moses created the Algebra Project, a mathematics literacy program that helps students in underserved communities develop skills for college and for the challenges of the technological world.

We shall overcome . . .

Dave Dennis is the director of the Southern Initiative of the Algebra Project.

We shall overcome . . .

Sheyann Webb-Christburg founded KEEP Productions Youth Development and Modeling Program, which helps youngsters acquire the skills and self-esteem they need to become leaders in their communities.

FRED SHUTTLESWORTH

BOB MOSES

DAVE DENNIS

SHEYANN WEBB-CHRISTBURG

IMPORTANT DATES

May 17, 1954. *Brown v. Board of Education of Topeka, Kansas,* outlaws segregation in public schools.

July 11, 1954. The White Citizens Council forms in Mississippi.

August 28, 1955. Emmett Till is lynched.

December 5, 1955. The Montgomery Bus Boycott is launched.

February 3, 1956. Autherine Lucy is admitted to the University of Alabama under court order.

January 10–11, 1957. The Southern Christian Leadership Conference (SCLC) is formed.

August 29, 1957. The 1957 Civil Rights Act declares disenfranchisement of black Americans illegal.

September 1957. Nine black students enroll at Central High School, Little Rock, Arkansas.

June 26, 1959. White officials close Prince Edward County, Virginia, public schools rather than integrate.

February 1, 1960. College students in Greensboro, North Carolina, stage a sit-in.

February 18, 1960. Nashville students sit in at lunch counters.

April 17, 1960. The Student Nonviolent Coordinating Committee (SNCC) is established.

May 9, 1960. The 1960 Voting Rights Act gives added protection to black Americans trying to vote.

November 7, 1960. The Albany Movement begins its six-year fight for integration.

May 4, 1961. The Freedom Rides begin.

August 1961. SNCC begins the Voter Education Project in McComb, Mississippi.

November 1, 1961. The Interstate Commerce Commission ends segregation in interstate bus travel.

September 29, 1962. James Meredith becomes the first black student at the University of Mississippi.

May 2, 1963. Children begin their demonstrations in Birmingham, Alabama.

June 12, 1963. Medgar Evers is murdered in Jackson, Mississippi.

August 28, 1963. More than 250,000 people participate in the March on Washington.

September 15, 1963. Four young girls are killed in the bombing of a Birmingham church.

November 3–5, 1963. The Council of Federated Organizations (COFO) holds a freedom vote in Mississippi.

November 22, 1963. President John F. Kennedy is assassinated.

January 23, 1964. The Twenty-fourth Amendment, eliminating the poll tax, is ratified.

April 26, 1964. The Mississippi Freedom Democratic Party (MFDP) is founded.

June 21, 1964. James Chaney, Michael Schwerner, and Andrew Goodman are murdered.

July 2, 1964. President Johnson signs the 1964 Civil Rights Act, prohibiting discrimination in public accommodations and in employment.

July–August 1964. COFO coordinates the Mississippi Freedom Summer.

August 1964. The MFDP is refused seating at the Democratic Convention.

February 21, 1965. Malcolm X is assassinated in New York City.

March 1965. Police attack demonstrators in Selma, Alabama.

August 6, 1965. The 1965 Voting Rights Act is signed into law.

ARTIST'S NOTE

History, to me, is an odd and amorphous construct that people tend to compartmentalize and call their own, when in fact it is our own. The word *history* itself is suspect. If you break the word down, it can be read as "his story." For the sake of how I feel, let's rename it "ourstory." It's easy to forget that, while individual stories are unfolding, a parallel "ourstory" is evolving. We are all connected, and the joy and pain that visits others will visit us because it is our joy and pain.

Growing up in a racially mixed family, I had the unique opportunity to sample the cultures of two distinct groups. Society may try to categorize me as African American because of my skin tone, but do I ignore who I truly am because others can't see it? Through Doreen Rappaport's efforts and words I have learned about the person I am, but more important, I have learned about the people we all are. In the case of the author-illustrator union, when one person appears European American (white) and one person appears African American (black), what we have forged is truly a telling of "ourstory."

Using the medium of expression that I love to bring to life the struggles of our people is a blessing in itself. Some of the struggles and conflicts cited in this book could not even have been visualized and expressed by the people who lived them not so long ago. I don't have to reach that far back in "mystory" to touch those — my mother, my father, my family — who fought for me and the opportunities I have, and I am grateful.

In this "politically correct" world, it is easy to lose sight of the fact that we continue to be divided by boundaries of our own making. We continually fail to realize that we are all simply human. So as you read the words and gaze at the images in this "ourstory," put yourselves in the shoes of these people who fought and loved so hard, for they are all of us.

Many blessings,

Shane W. Evans

Acknowledgments

I thank the reference librarians at the Schomburg Center for Black Culture; Sharon Harrison and Andrea Tompa for their research skills; Carol Briggs, head librarian, and the volunteers at Roeliff Jansen Community Library for procuring essential interlibrary loans; Cecile Proverbs for her superb copyediting skills; Sherry Fatla for her exquisite graphic design; and Mendy Samstein, Dorothy Carter, Professor Emeritas of Children's Literature, Bank Street College of Education, and Eli Zaretsky, professor of history at the New School University, for critiquing the manuscript.

My deepest gratitude to my editor, Mary Lee Donovan, whose passion for all three books and commitment to excellence pushed this writer to new places.

—

Source Notes and Permissions

The books and articles listed in the Bibliography were all invaluable sources in my research. A few clarifying notes:

My accounts of the actions, feelings, and dialogue of Elizabeth Eckford, Fannie Lou Hamer, James Lawson, John Lewis, Diane Nash, Rosa Parks, Jo Ann Robinson, Sheyann Webb, and Mose Wright all come directly from first-person narratives.

The quotes from Louis Armstrong, Benjamin Mays, Chester Himes, Esther Mae Scott, and James Yates on page 6 were taken from Leon F. Litwack's extraordinary book, *Trouble in Mind: Black Southerners in the Age of Jim Crow*. New York: Vintage, 1998.

The excerpt from "For My People" by Margaret Walker on page 5 was originally published in *Poetry: A Magazine of Verse*, Volume LI No. II (November 1937). 81–83.

On page 25, James Lawson reads from the New Testament, Luke, chapter 4, verses 17-19.

The quote from James Farmer on page 35 was excerpted from *Voices of Freedom*, by Henry Hampton and Steve Fayer, with Sarah Flynn. New York: Bantam, 1990.

Joyce Brown's poem on page 50 was printed in the August 5, 1964, edition of *The Student Voice*, the newsletter of SNCC (the Student Nonviolent Coordinating Committee).

I am grateful for permission to reprint the following, listed in order of appearance in the book:

Page 23
Excerpt from Langston Hughes's "Week by Week" column on James Farmer, published in the *Chicago Defender* (June 14, 1958). Used with permission of the *Chicago Defender*.

Page 33
"Keep Your Eyes on the Prize." Adaptation of traditional song by Alice Wine and members of SNCC. From the Oak Publication *We Shall Overcome*, compiled and edited by Guy and Candie Carawan. Copyright © 1963 (Renewed) by Oak Publications. International Copyright Secured. All Rights Reserved. Reprinted by Permission.

Page 39
"Oh Freedom." Adaptation of traditional song by members of SNCC (the Student Nonviolent Coordinating Committee). From the Oak Publication *We Shall Overcome*, compiled and edited by Guy and Candie Carawan. Copyright © 1963 (Renewed) by Oak Publications. International Copyright Secured. All Rights Reserved. Reprinted by Permission.

Page 41
"We Shall Overcome." Musical and lyrical adaptation by Zilphia Horton, Frank Hamilton, Guy Carawan, and Pete Seeger. Inspired by African American gospel singing; members of the Food & Tobacco Workers Union, Charleston, SC; and the southern

BIBLIOGRAPHY

Bates, Daisy. *The Long Shadow of Little Rock.* Fayetteville: University of Arkansas, 1986.

Cagin, Seth, and Philip Dray. *We Are Not Afraid.* New York: Bantam, 1988.

Dittmer, John. *Local People: The Struggle for Civil Rights in Mississippi.* Urbana and Chicago: University of Illinois Press, 1994.

Halberstam, David. *The Children.* New York: Random House, 1998.

Hamer, Fannie Lou. *To Praise Our Bridges: An Autobiography.* Jackson, Miss.: KIPCO, 1967.

Levine, Lawrence W. *Black Culture and Black Consciousness.* Oxford, London, and New York: Oxford University Press, 1977.

Lewis, John, with Michael D'Orso. *Walking with the Wind: A Memoir of the Movement.* New York: Simon and Schuster, 1998.

Metress, Christopher, ed. *A Documentary Narrative: The Lynching of Emmett Till.* Charlottesville: University of Virginia Press, 2002.

Moody, Anne. *Coming of Age in Mississippi.* New York: Dell, 1968.

Robinson, Jo Ann Gibson. *The Montgomery Bus Boycott and the Women Who Started It: The Memoir of Jo Ann Gibson Robinson.* Knoxville: University of Tennessee Press, 1987.

Webb, Sheyann, and Rachel Nelson West, as told to Frank Sinkora. *Selma, Lord, Selma: Girlhood Memories of Civil Rights Days.* Tuscaloosa: University of Alabama Press, 1988.

Whitfield, Stephen J. *A Death in the Delta: The Story of Emmett Till.* New York: Free Press, 1988.

Wilkins, Roy, with Tom Matthews. *Standing Fast: The Autobiography of Roy Wilkins.* New York: Viking, 1982.

To learn more about the civil rights movement, you can read:

Adoff, Arnold. *Malcolm X*. Illustrated by Rudy Gutierrez. New York: HarperCollins Children's Books, 1999.

Andryszewski, Tricia. *The March on Washington, 1963: Gathering to Be Heard*. Brookfield, Conn.: Millbrook Press, 1996.

Archer, Jules. *They Had a Dream: The Civil Rights Struggle from Frederick Douglass to Marcus Garvey to Martin Luther King, Jr. and Malcolm X*. New York: Penguin Putnam Books for Young Readers, 1996.

Bridges, Ruby, and Margo Lundell. *Through My Eyes*. New York: Scholastic, 1999.

Colman, Penny. *Fannie Lou Hamer and the Fight for the Vote*. Brookfield, Conn.: Millbrook Press, 1993.

Crowe, Chris. *Getting Away with Murder: The True Story of the Emmett Till Case*. New York: Phyllis Fogelman Books, 2003.

Haskins, Jim. *The March on Washington*. New York: HarperCollins, 1993.

Hill, Christine M. *John Lewis: From Freedom Rider to Congressman*. New Jersey: Enslow, 2002.

Jakoubek, Robert E. *James Farmer and the Freedom Rides*. Brookfield, Conn.: Millbrook Press, 1994.

King, Casey, and Linda Barrett Osborne. *Oh, Freedom! Kids Talk about the Civil Rights Movement with the People Who Made It Happen*. Illustrated by Joe Brooks. New York: Random House, 1997.

Levine, Ellen. *If You Lived at the Time of Martin Luther King*. Illustrated by Anna Rich. New York: Scholastic, 1990.

———. *Freedom's Children*. New York: Puffin, 2000.

McWhorter, Diane. *A Dream of Freedom: The Civil Rights Movement from 1964 to 1968*. New York: Scholastic, 2004.

Meltzer, Milton. *There Comes a Time: The Struggle for Civil Rights*. New York: Random House, 2001.

Mills, Kay. *This Little Light of Mine: The Life of Fannie Lou Hamer*. New York: Dutton/Plume, 1994.

Myers, Walter Dean. *The Greatest: Muhammad Ali*. New York: Scholastic, 2001.

Parks, Rosa, with Jim Haskins. *Rosa Parks: My Story*. New York: Puffin, 1992.

Rappaport, Doreen. *Martin's Big Words: The Life of Dr. Martin Luther King, Jr.* Illustrated by Bryan Collier. New York: Jump at the Sun/Hyperion Books for Children, 2001.

———. *The School Is Not White! A True Story of the Civil Rights Movement*. Illustrated by Curtis James. New York: Jump at the Sun/Hyperion Books for Children, 2005.

A NOTE ABOUT WEBSITES

The Internet has thousands of sites on the civil rights movement and the people involved in it. Use caution when evaluating the information on any site. Many sites are not "official" or authorized. Sites sponsored by museums, organizations, and national parks are usually trustworthy.

INDEX

For Mendy Samstein and Nancy Cooper Samstein, with love and admiration
D. R.

Thank you, God.
I dedicate this book to my friends and brothers, Gino M. and Charles W.
Thank you for your inspiration.
S. W. E.

First paperback edition 2008

The Library of Congress has cataloged the hardcover edition as follows:

Rappaport, Doreen
Nobody gonna turn me 'round : stories and songs of the civil rights movement /
Doreen Rappaport ; illustrated by Shane W. Evans
p. cm.
The third book in a trilogy, which began with No more! (2002) and Free at last! (2004).
ISBN 978-0-7636-1927-5 (hardcover)
1. African Americans — Civil rights — History — 20th century — Miscellanea — Juvenile literature.
2. Civil rights movements — United States — History — 20th century — Miscellanea — Juvenile literature.
3. United States — Race relations — Miscellanea — Juvenile literature.
I. Evans, Shane, ill. II. Title.
E185.61.R236 2006
323.1196'073009046 — dc22 2005053184

ISBN 978-0-7636-3892-4 (paperback)

15 16 17 18 APS 10 9 8 7 6 5
Printed in Humen, Dongguan, China

This book was typeset in Integrity.
The illustrations were done in oil.

Candlewick Press
99 Dover Street
Somerville, Massachusetts 02144

visit us at www.candlewick.com